# 100 Things
## you should know about
# Warriors

# 100 Things
## you should know about
# Warriors

John Malam

Consultant: Philip Steele

**MASON CREST PUBLISHERS INC.**
**370 Reed Road**
**Broomall, Pennsylvania 19008**
**(866)MCP-BOOK (toll free)**
**www.masoncrest.com**

ISBN: 978-1-4222-1979-9
Series ISBN (15 titles): 978-1-4222-1964-5

First Printing
9 8 7 6 5 4 3 2 1

Cataloging-in-Publication Data on file with the Library of Congress.
Printed in the U.S.A.

First published in 2010 by Miles Kelly Publishing Ltd
Bardfield Centre, Great Bardfield, Essex, CM7 4SL, UK

**Editorial Director:** Belinda Gallagher

**Art Director:** Jo Brewer

**Managing Editor:** Rosie McGuire

**Assistant Editor:** Claire Philip

**Senior Designer:** Simon Lee

**Volume Designer:** Andrea Slane

**Image Manager:** Liberty Newton

**Indexer:** Eleanor Holme

**Production Manager:** Elizabeth Brunwin

**Reprographics:** Anthony Cambray, Stephan Davis, Ian Paulyn

**ACKNOWLEDGEMENTS**
The publishers would like to thank the following artists
who have contributed to this book:

Julian Baker (JB Illustrations), Mike Foster (Maltings Partnership),
Mariusz Kozik, Mike White (Temple Rogers)
Cover artwork: Mariusz Kozik

All other artworks are from the Miles Kelly Artwork Bank

The publishers would like to thank the following sources
for the use of their photographs:

t = top, b = bottom, l = left, r = right, c = centre

Pages 2–3 iñaki antoñana plaza/iStockphoto.com; 6–7 Warner Bros. Pictures/Moviestore Collection Ltd;
8(bc) Jim Cole/Alamy; 15(r) Warner Bros. Pictures/Moviestore Collection Ltd; 16–17 Warner Bros. Pictures/TopFoto;
17(tr) North Wind Picture Archives/Alamy, (br)Alfio Ferlito/Fotolia; 27(b) Twentieth Century-Fox Film Corporation/
Moviestore Collection Ltd; 31 Gianni Dagli Orti/Corbis; 32–33 Barry Lewis/Corbis; 32(tr) North Wind Picture Archives/Alamy;
34(br) PoodlesRock/Corbis; 35 TopFoto/HIP; 36(tr) Constance McGuire/iStockphoto.com; 38(tr) The British Library/HIP;
40(tl) HultonArchive/iStockphoto.com; 40–41 Bogdan Willewalde/Getty Images; 42–43 Rajesh Jantilal/AFP/Getty Images;
43(tl) The Granger Collection/TopFoto; 44 Bettmann/Corbis; 44–45(tc) Corbis; 46(l) New Line Cinema/Moviestore Collection Ltd;
46–47 Lucasfilm/Moviestore Collection Ltd; 47(br) Twentieth Century-Fox Film Corporation/Moviestore Collection Ltd

All other photographs are from:

iStockphoto.com, ImageState, PhotoSphere

Every effort has been made to acknowledge the source and copyright holder of each picture.

# Contents

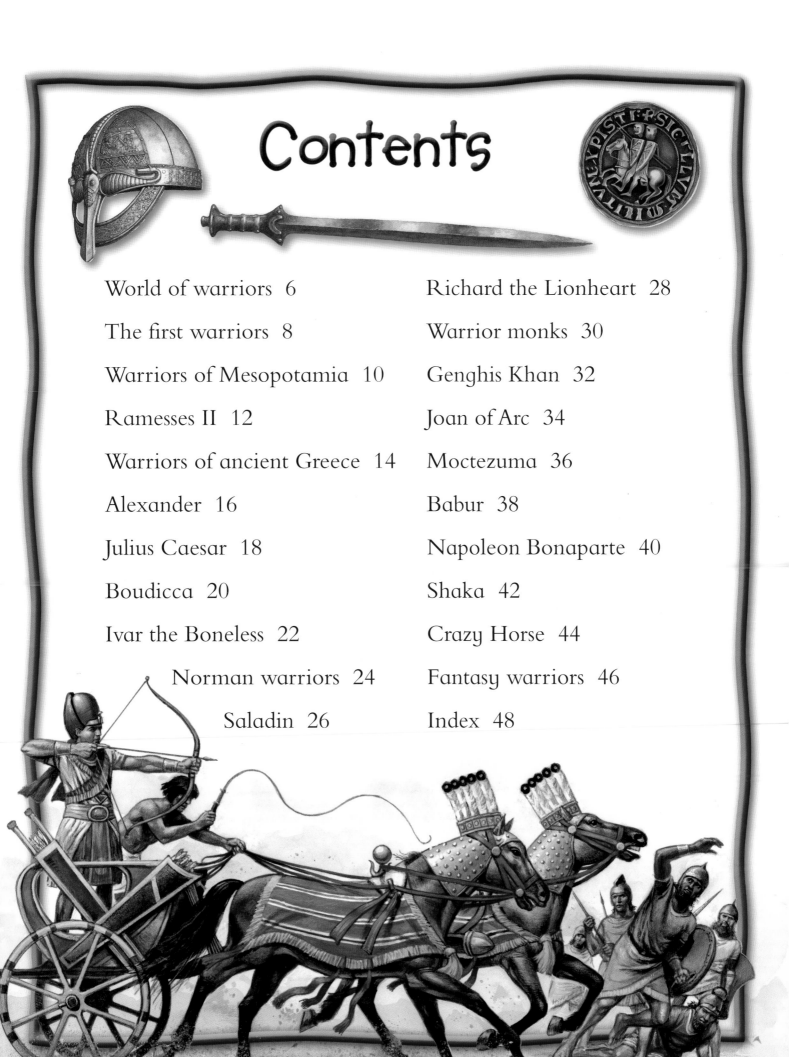

# World of warriors

**1** Warriors are people who fight in battles. A warrior is often a soldier or trained fighter who has shown great courage. Great warriors have the power to capture our imagination. Throughout history to the present day the cry of the warrior has been heard around the world.

▼ The ancient Greeks believed that a war was fought in the 1200s BCE between the Greeks and the Trojans. In the story, Hector, a Trojan warrior, killed Patroclus, a Greek hero.

# The first warriors

**2** **The earliest warriors lived in prehistoric times.** Archaeologists divide prehistory into three ages. First the Stone Age, when stone was used to make tools and weapons. Then the Bronze Age, when metal was first used. After this came the Iron Age, when iron took over from bronze.

▲ The first axes were made from stone, such as flint. Flint axes were shaped from large blocks, and had very sharp cutting edges.

**3** **Prehistoric people used a range of weapons.** Many axes, sling stones, arrows, swords and daggers survive today, but weapons made of perishable materials, such as wood, rotted away long ago. From the weapons that have survived, we can tell that prehistoric people lived in violent times.

**4** **The first warriors must have been brave.** A fighter may have had to prove his bravery before becoming a warrior. He may have been set challenges to test his courage, or have been made to perform tasks in a ceremony. Only by passing the tests would he have been accepted as a warrior by the rest of his group.

◄ ► Weapons of prehistoric warriors —a spear, an axe and a sword.

Iron sword

Stone spear

Bronze axe

## QUIZ

1. What are the three ages of prehistory?
2. Which metal took over from bronze?
3. How many arrowheads were found at Crickley Hill?

Answers:
1. Stone Age, Bronze Age, Iron Age
2. Iron, 3. More than 400

8

## PREHISTORIC TIMELINE

The division of prehistory into three main ages is based on the technology of each period.

| 1,000,000–8500 BCE | 8500–7000 BCE | 7000–2750 BCE | 2750–750 BCE | 750–50 BCE |
|---|---|---|---|---|
| Palaeolithic or Old Stone Age | Mesolithic or Middle Stone Age | Neolithic or New Stone Age | Bronze Age | Iron Age |

**5** **Prehistoric battles were fought for many reasons.** Rivalries between groups might have been a good reason to go to war, so arguments over who owned land and other property may have led to battles. If different people in a group wanted to be leader, the only way to decide may have been to fight it out.

**6** **An arrow battle was fought in prehistoric times at Crickley Hill, in Gloucestershire, England.** On top of the hill is a Neolithic (New Stone Age) camp. Archaeologists found more than 400 flint arrowheads scattered around the two entrances to the camp. It seems the camp was the site of full-scale arrow battle, about 4,500 years ago.

▶ A prehistoric hunting party equipped with bows and spears.

# Warriors of Mesopotamia

**7** The first armies were in Mesopotamia—a region of the Middle East where present-day Iran and Iraq are found. Here, men were first organized into fighting forces around 4,500 years ago. Kings wanted to show power, and controlling an army was a way to do this. King Sargon (2334–2279 BCE) was the first Mesopotamian ruler to have a full-time army.

▲ Mesopotamia was an area of the Middle East between the rivers Euphrates and Tigris.

## I DON'T BELIEVE IT!

Using a composite bow, a Mesopotamian archer could fire an arrow up to about 800 feet (245 meters).

**8** Mesopotamian armies had hundreds of thousands of troops. They were organized into foot soldiers (infantry), horse soldiers (cavalry) and the most feared of all—charioteers. Chariots were wheeled, horse-drawn platforms for archers to shoot arrows from. Some battles involved hundreds of chariots.

▲ Mounted archers were a rapid strike force of Assyrian armies. Assyria was a kingdom of northern Mesopotamia.

**10** The Battle of Carchemish was fought in 605 BCE. It was between the Babylonians (one of the peoples of Mesopotamia) and the ancient Egyptians. The Babylonian army destroyed the Egyptian army, and the surviving Egyptian forces fled. The Babylonians gave chase, and a second battle took place near the Sea of Galilee, in Palestine. The Egyptians were defeated again, and retreated into Egypt.

**11** Mesopotamian myths tell of warrior heroes. The greatest was Gilgamesh who, according to legend, defeated evil monsters. On a quest for immortality (eternal life), Gilgamesh was given a test to stay awake for seven nights. But he fell asleep, failing the test, and so never became immortal.

▶ In the legend of Gilgamesh, the warrior Gilgamesh killed a hideous giant called Humbaba.

**9** The Mesopotamian warrior's main weapon was the bow. At first, bows were made from single pieces of wood, but then people discovered how to make bows from layers of wood and bone glued together. These were called composite bows, and they fired arrows further than one-piece bows.

# Ramesses II

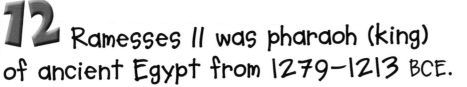

**12** Ramesses II was pharaoh (king) of ancient Egypt from 1279–1213 BCE. Ramesses was one of Egypt's greatest warrior pharaohs, and because he conquered Egypt's enemies he became known as Ramesses the Great. He is best known for leading his forces against the Hittites in the Battle of Kadesh.

**13** The army of Ramesses II had about 20,000 warriors. Armies were organized into divisions of about 5,000 men, who were mostly infantry soldiers. There were also charioteers, who steered chariots as their passengers shot arrows or threw spears. Chariots caused panic, smashing through enemy front lines at up to 24 miles (38 kilometers) per hour.

◀ Stone statues of Ramesses II were put up all over ancient Egypt.

## QUIZ

1. In what year did Ramesses II become pharaoh?
2. What was the top speed of an Egyptian chariot?
3. Where did the Hittites come from?
4. When was the Battle of Kadesh?
5. What was the outcome of the Battle of Kadesh?

Answers:
1. 1279 BCE
2. About 24 miles per hour
3. Turkey  4. 1275 BCE  5. A draw

◀ Egyptian charioteers were skilled warriors and struck fear into the enemy.

**14** Egyptian infantry soldiers fought with spears, axes, curved swords and daggers. Archers used powerful bows that shot arrows tipped with points of chipped stone. Instead of wearing armor, warriors protected themselves with leather or wooden shields.

**15** Before Ramesses II, Tuthmosis III waged war against Egypt's neighbors to the northeast. Tuthmosis was very successful, but the Hittites (a warlike people from an area that is now Turkey) also wanted to control this region, and they became Egypt's bitter enemies.

**16** Ramesses II fought the Hittites in 1275 BCE at Kadesh (in modern-day Syria) because the Hittites were threatening to invade Egypt. It was probably the largest chariot battle ever fought, involving 5,000–6,000 chariots. At first, the Hittites were winning, and the Egyptians retreated. Then Ramesses stopped the panic among his troops and fought back. The Hittites retreated into the city of Kadesh. Both sides claimed they had won.

▶ The Egyptian Empire stretched to the borders of present-day Turkey.

HITTITE EMPIRE

KADESH

MEDITERRANEAN SEA

MEMPHIS • HELIOPOLIS

HERAKLEOPOLIS

LIBYA                    ARABIA

NILE

THEBES

EGYPTIAN EMPIRE         RED SEA

ABU SIMBEL

# Warriors of ancient Greece

**17** Foot soldiers called hoplites formed the core of every ancient Greek army. Each of the city-states of Greece had its own army of fighting men. Rival cities went to war on many occasions, but they also came together to fight a common enemy, usually the Persians.

▲ Ancient Greece was divided into city-states. Each one was a city and the surrounding territory.

GREECE

• CORINTH    • ATHENS

• OLYMPIA

IONIAN SEA

• SPARTA

► A hoplite was named after his hoplon (shield).

Helmet

Spear

Linen corselet

Short sword

Shield (hoplon)

Greave

**18** A hoplite carried a large round shield, a long spear and a short sword. His body armor was a bronze helmet, a stiff linen corselet (tunic), and bronze greaves (leg guards). This was the standard equipment for all hoplites, regardless of their city-state.

**19** Battles took place on flat, open plains. Hoplite ranks stood in a formation called a phalanx. It was six to eight ranks deep, with hundreds of men in each rank. The phalanxes marched toward each other, with the first three ranks holding their spears level, pointing at the enemy.

◄ When armies met, the front soldiers thrust their spears into each other's phalanx, while the men at the back pushed their comrades forward.

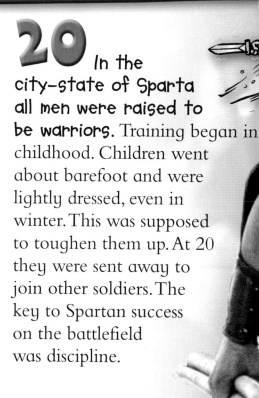

**20** In the city-state of Sparta all men were raised to be warriors. Training began in childhood. Children went about barefoot and were lightly dressed, even in winter. This was supposed to toughen them up. At 20 they were sent away to join other soldiers. The key to Spartan success on the battlefield was discipline.

▶ The warrior Achilles, as seen in the film *Troy* (Warner Brothers, 2004). He was one of the greatest heroes of ancient Greece.

**21** Achilles was a mythological Greek warrior. As a baby, his mother took him by the heel and dipped him in the River Styx. The only part of him untouched by the water was his heel. The river's magical waters gave him great strength but his undipped heel was his weak spot. Achilles fought in the war against the Trojans. He defeated Hector, their champion fighter, and seemed unstoppable. He was only killed when an arrow struck him in the heel.

# Alexander

**22** Alexander the Great (356–323 BCE) was one of the most brilliant warriors of all time. He came from Macedonia, a region in the north of Greece. In 11 remarkable years his army conquered land from Greece to the Indus River, Pakistan. It was the greatest empire of the ancient world.

**23** Alexander tamed a wild stallion when he was just nine years old. He noticed the horse was afraid of its own shadow, so he turned it to face the sun, so its shadow was behind it. The horse became calm and allowed Alexander to mount him. Alexander named the horse Bucephalus, and rode it into many battles.

▲ Alexander and Bucephalus, as shown in the film *Alexander* (Warner Brothers, 2004). The name Bucephalus meant "ox head," in reference to a mark on its skin.

**24** Macedonia became powerful during the reign of Alexander's father, Philip II. In 338 BCE, Alexander led the Macedonians to victory at the Battle of Chaeronea. King Philip next planned to free Greek cities in Asia Minor (Turkey) from Persian rule. When his father died, Alexander decided to carry out his plans.

**25** Alexander raised an army of 43,000 hoplites and 5,500 cavalry. Soon after entering the Persian Empire, Alexander's army defeated a Persian army at the Battle of the Granicus River (334 BCE). This opened the way to the Greek cities of Asia Minor, which Alexander freed from Persian control.

▶ The Battle of the Granicus River was fought in present-day Turkey.

**26** Alexander's greatest battle against the Persians was the Battle of Issus in 333 BCE. His army of 35,000 troops met the army of Darius III, king of Persia, at Issus, in modern-day southern Turkey. Alexander's army was victorious, despite being outnumbered two to one. Later that year he defeated them at the Battle of Gaugamela (in present-day Iraq). Then Alexander led his army into the heart of the Persian Empire, taking city after city.

▶ A mosaic of the Battle of Issus, showing Darius III and his army.

## I DON'T BELIEVE IT!

Alexander the Great marched a massive total of around 20,000 miles (32,000 kilometers) over the course of his 11-year battle campaign.

# Julius Caesar

▼ A Roman warship was a long, thin galley ship. It used oarsmen to row it through the water.

**27** **Julius Caesar (100–44 BCE) was the greatest Roman general.** He was highly successful, defeating the Gauls (tribes that lived in present-day France and Belgium) and invading Britain in 55 BCE and 54 BCE. Caesar then led his troops into Italy and fought a civil war to rule the Roman world. He won, and was made "dictator for life," but was stabbed to death in 44 BCE.

**28** **As a young man, Caesar was captured by pirates.** He was caught when sailing to the Mediterranean island of Rhodes. The pirates held him until a ransom was paid. Caesar vowed to hunt the pirates down. All of them were found and executed on his orders.

**29** **Caesar led the best army of the time.** Roman soldiers (legionaries) were armed with a dagger, a short sword and a javelin. They wore helmets and armor made from metal and leather and carried shields. For long-distance fighting, a *ballista* fired big arrows with iron tips. In siege warfare an *onager* hurled rocks onto enemy defenses.

## I DON'T BELIEVE IT!

A skeleton from Maiden Castle in Dorset, England, had a ballista bolt in its spine—evidence of a battle between Britons and Romans.

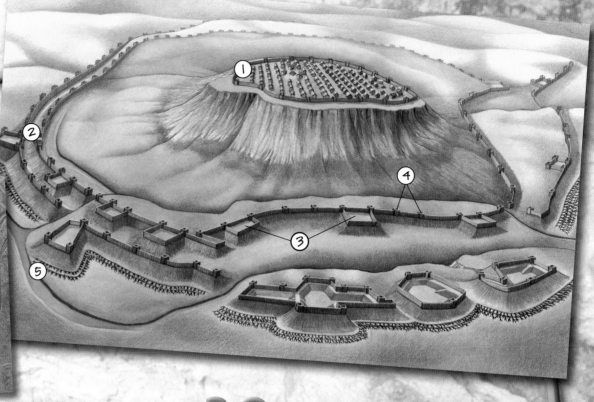

► Caesar's plan at Alesia was to starve the Gauls into surrender. It worked.

## Key

1 Hilltop fort of Alesia

2 First ditch and wall traps Gauls

3 Roman camps

4 Roman look-out points

5 Second ditch and wall keeps Romans safe

▼ Roman legionaries (soldiers) preparing a ballista to fire a bolt.

**30** Caesar led his army into Gaul, planning to make it part of the Roman world. For seven years, battles were fought between the Romans and the tribes of Gaul. When a group of tribes (led by the Gallic chief Vercingetorix) rebelled, Caesar took action to end the revolt.

**31** Vercingetorix led an army of Gauls against the Romans in 52 BCE. The Romans forced the Gauls back to their hilltop fortress at Alesia, France. Caesar's troops encircled the hill with huge ditches. One kept the Gauls trapped inside, and the other protected the Romans from the Gauls' allies. Realizing that he could not win, Vercingetorix surrendered.

19

# Boudicca

**32** **Boudicca was a warrior queen.** She was from a Celtic tribe called the Iceni, which lived in the east of Britain. A Roman writer described Boudicca as tall, with long red hair, and wearing a large gold necklace. Boudicca is famous for leading an uprising against the Romans.

**33** **Boudicca's husband, King Prasutagus, died around 60 CE.** He left half his kingdom to the Romans and the other half to Boudicca. The Romans wanted all of it, and set about taking it by force. So during 60 CE and 61 CE, Boudicca led the Iceni and other British tribes in a rebellion against the Romans.

▶ Boudicca, warrior queen of the Iceni, fought the Romans in Britain.

**I DON'T BELIEVE IT!**
Underneath Colchester, London and St. Albans, there is still a thick layer of burned earth, left from Boudicca's attacks on them.

**34** **Boudicca is said to have led more than 100,000 warriors against the Romans.** Known as the Britons, they fought with swords and spears, and protected themselves with shields. Some rode into battle in chariots. They were brave warriors, but were not as organized as the Romans.

**35** Boudicca's warriors went south, to the Roman towns of southeast Britain. They burned the towns of Camulodunum (Colchester), Londinium (London) and Verulamium (St. Albans), killing some 70,000 civilians and destroying the Roman IXth Legion.

**36** Boudicca's last battle was somewhere in the English Midlands. As many as 230,000 Britons fought a smaller Roman force. The Romans had better tactics and weapons, and 80,000 Britons are said to have died. The Romans won, and Boudicca died soon after the battle, possibly ending her own life with poison.

# Ivar the Boneless

**37** Ivar Ragnarsson was a Viking warrior from Scandinavia, in northern Europe. His nickname was "Ivar the Boneless," which may have been linked to a Viking story about a man whose bones shriveled because he had done something really bad. Ivar was a leader of the Great Army, a force of Vikings that invaded England in 865 CE.

**38** Ivar the Boneless was a berserker — the bravest of all Viking warriors. Berserkers worked themselves up in preparation for battle by shouting and biting the edges of their shields. They wore no armor and felt they had the strength of wild beasts. The word "beserker" is the origin of the expression "to go berserk."

▲ A figure of a berserker biting his shield.

**39** Viking warbands struck fear into the people of western and northern Europe. In November 866 CE, the Viking Great Army captured the Anglo-Saxon town of York in northern England. Ivar was probably one of the warriors who helped take the town. York became the capital of the Viking kingdom in England.

▼ Viking warriors traveled in longships. These could be rowed inland along rivers.

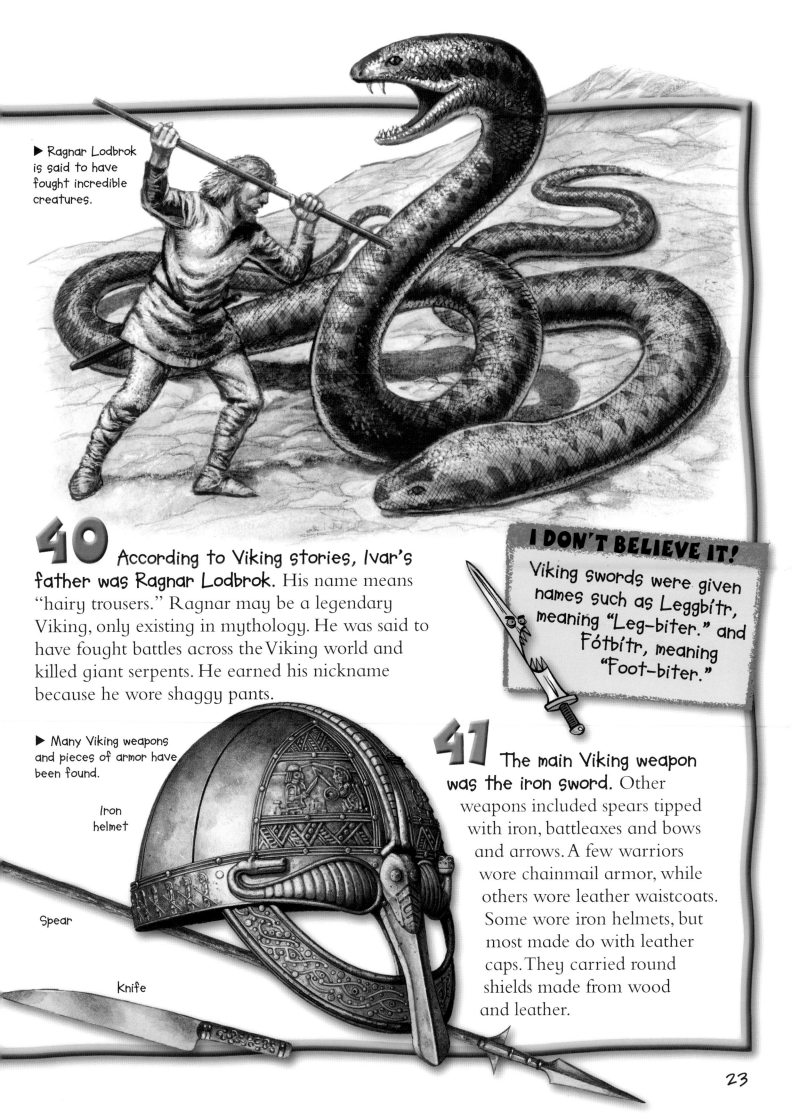

▶ Ragnar Lodbrok is said to have fought incredible creatures.

# 40

**According to Viking stories, Ivar's father was Ragnar Lodbrok.** His name means "hairy trousers." Ragnar may be a legendary Viking, only existing in mythology. He was said to have fought battles across the Viking world and killed giant serpents. He earned his nickname because he wore shaggy pants.

## I DON'T BELIEVE IT!

Viking swords were given names such as Leggbítr, meaning "Leg-biter." and Fótbítr, meaning "Foot-biter."

▶ Many Viking weapons and pieces of armor have been found.

Iron helmet

Spear

Knife

# 41

**The main Viking weapon was the iron sword.** Other weapons included spears tipped with iron, battleaxes and bows and arrows. A few warriors wore chainmail armor, while others wore leather waistcoats. Some wore iron helmets, but most made do with leather caps. They carried round shields made from wood and leather.

# Norman warriors

**42** In 911 CE, a Viking warband led by Rollo arrived in northern France. At first the region was known as *Nordmannia* ("Northman's Land"). The Vikings settled in the area and it became known as Normandy. The warriors who came from this area were the Normans.

▲ In 1066, the Normans departed from St. Valery in northern France and landed at Pevensey in southern England, ready to do battle.

**43** The Normans were skilled fighters, organizers and builders. In the 1000s CE, Norman armies conquered England, much of France, southern Italy and Sicily. They took part in the Crusades to the Holy Land (Palestine), and built many strong buildings.

**44** A Norman army was made up of many foot soldiers. They fought with spears, axes and bows. The cavalry was the strongest part of the army. Cavalry soldiers owned their own horses and went to war in the hope of being rewarded for their service.

**45** In battle, Norman foot soldiers formed themselves into defensive shield walls or war hedges. The front ranks held their long shields close together, forming a solid barrier that protected the warriors behind it from missiles. The shield wall came apart to allow the fighters to use their weapons, and for the cavalry to charge through.

**46** On September 28, 1066, William, Duke of Normandy invaded England. He led about 750 ships across the English Channel from France. On board was an army of 10,000 men and 3,000 horses. On October 14, 1066, the Normans defeated the English in the Battle of Hastings. Harold, the king of England, was killed, and William became England's first Norman king. He was known as William the Conqueror.

◀ At Senlac Hill, near Hastings, Norman soldiers charged uphill to attack the English.

## QUIZ

1. What area of France did the Normans come from?
2. What was the strongest part of a Norman army?
3. In what year was the Battle of Hastings?

Answers:
1. Normandy
2. The cavalry 3. 1066

# Saladin

**47** Saladin (1137–1193) was a Muslim warrior. He led a religious war (*jihad*) in the Middle East. Saladin (or Salah ad-Din Yuseuf) became a soldier at 14, and for many years fought against other Muslims in Egypt. By 1187, he had become the sultan (ruler) of Egypt and Syria, and decided to drive Christians out of the holy city of Jerusalem.

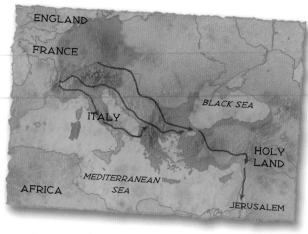

▲ Both sides used mounted troops in their battles.

▲ Routes taken by Crusader armies as they travlled to the Holy Land.

**48** The Battle of Hattin was fought in July, 1187. It was a major battle between Muslims, led by Saladin, and Christians, led by Guy of Lusignan, and took place near Lake Tiberias in northern Palestine. Guy had about 20,000 troops, but Saladin's army was half as big again. Perhaps as few as 3,000 Christian warriors survived the battle. It was an important victory for Saladin.

◀ Muslim warriors were lightly armored and fought with curved swords.

**49** The series of religious wars fought in the Holy Land (Palestine) between Muslims and Christians were called Crusades. Between 1096 and 1291, Christian soldiers traveled from Europe to the Holy Land, where they fought to curb the spread of Islam, save Jerusalem, and protect Christian pilgrims who went there.

**50** After the Battle of Hattin, Saladin conquered Christian strongholds in the Holy Land. He took Acre and Jaffa in present-day Israel, and Beirut in Lebanon. By September 1187 his army reached Jerusalem. The Christians surrendered after a short siege. Saladin showed some mercy, allowing some Christians to leave the city in return for a ransom. The rest he sold into slavery.

**51** Saladin's warriors were mostly lightly armed mounted archers. They wore little body armor, so they could ride much faster than their Christian foes who wore heavy metal armor. Speed was the Muslim warriors' secret of success. They preferred to engage in skirmishes, picking off their enemies with well-aimed arrows before making their escape. This way, they weakened their opponents.

▶ The forces of Saladin's army besiege the city of Jerusalem in 1187, as shown in the film *Kingdom of Heaven* (Twentieth Century Fox, 2005).

# Richard the Lionheart

**52** King Richard I (1157–1199) was king of England for ten years, from 1189 to 1199. He was known as *Coeur de Lion*, or Richard the Lionheart, because of his success as a military leader and warrior.

► King Richard I led an army of crusaders to the Holy Land.

**53** Richard, the Holy Roman Emperor Frederick I (king of Germany and Italy), and King Philip II of France organized a crusade to free Jerusalem from Saladin. This was the Third Crusade, and lasted from 1189 to 1192. On reaching the Holy Land, the first action of Richard's knights was to capture the city of Acre from the Muslims. He did this in July 1191, with the use of battering rams and catapults.

**54** After taking Acre, Richard marched toward Jerusalem. His progress was stopped in September 1191, when he fought Saladin at the Battle of Arsuf. The Christian and Muslim armies each had about 20,000 warriors, and although the battle was a victory for Richard, Saladin's army was able to regroup and continue with its hit-and-run skirmishes.

▼ King Richard's army besieged the city of Acre for about six weeks.

Catapult

Siege tower

Battering ram

**55** Richard came to within about 12 miles (19 kilometers) of Jerusalem. He was unable to attack it as his supplies were low and Saladin's constant skirmishes had picked off too many of his troops. The two leaders made peace, and in return for Richard agreeing to leave, Saladin allowed Christian pilgrims to visit Jerusalem, ending the Third Crusade.

**56** The crusaders set sail for home, but Richard's adventures weren't over. While traveling overland from Venice, he was captured by an Austrian enemy, and handed over to Henry VI of Germany. A ransom of 150,000 silver marks (a unit of currency) was demanded for his release. After being held for over a year, the ransom was paid, and Richard returned home.

# Warrior monks

**57** Crusader armies were composed of foot soldiers and mounted knights. Among the knights were warriors who belonged to religious groups or orders. They followed strict rules, and were organized in a similar way to monks in monasteries. These "warrior monks" were anything but peaceful.

## DESIGN A SHIELD

Medieval knights carried shields made of wood and covered with colored leather. They had pictures or patterns (coats of arms) on them so knights could recognize their friends in battle. Look for pictures of shields in books or on the Internet. Then have a go at drawing and coloring a design of your own.

**58** The Knights Hospitaller were founded in Jerusalem in 1099. At first their role was to provide safe lodgings for Christian pilgrims to the city, and to care for the sick and wounded in their hospital. This gradually became a sizeable military force, acting as armed guards for pilgrims and crusaders. The Knights Hospitaller were also known as the Knights of St. John.

▶ The symbol of the Knights Templar—two knights on one horse.

**59** The Knights Templar were founded in Jerusalem in 1119 by nine French knights. They were called Templars because their headquarters was a building on the site of the Temple of Solomon. Knights Templar were the best disciplined and bravest crusaders. They were also the richest, thanks to donations from Christians in Europe.

# 60

**The German Teutonic Knights were founded at Acre in 1198.** They were formed to protect Christian pilgrims, but took up arms against Muslims and built castles. Active in the Holy Land until the 1290s, their main work was carried out later in the Baltic region, fighting in Lithuania.

◀ Knights took part in jousting tournaments, charging at each other with lances.

# 61

**The armored knight was the elite warrior of medieval Europe.** In childhood he was taught to ride and to use a sword and lance. As a knight, he took part in tournaments to improve his fighting skills, ready for when he went to war.

▶ Knights marched with colorful pennants (triangular flags).

# Genghis Khan

**62** Mongol warrior Genghis Khan (1162–1227) ruled with great discipline. He was born in Mongolia, and given the name Temujin. The Mongols were one of many tribes that lived on the grassy plains (steppe) of central Asia. They were horsemen who followed their herds of grazing animals.

▲ Genghis Khan was a fearless warrior who led his Mongol troops to victory.

**63** **The Mongol tribes were constantly at war with each other.** Temujin set about uniting the tribes, and in 1206 he became ruler (*khan*) of them all. From then on he was known as Genghis Khan, meaning "Ruler of the Earth." His armies conquered almost all of China. By the time he died, his empire stretched from the Black Sea to the Pacific Ocean—it was the largest empire in history.

▶ The Mongol Empire covered much of Asia and beyond.

**64** **Mongol warriors wore leather armor and helmets and fired arrows from powerful bows as they rode.** Soldiers also carried swords, maces, axes and sometimes short spears with hooks on their points. Mongol warriors each had a string of horses, and changed their mounts often, so as not to tire them.

**65** **Mongol warriors were organized into large groups, which were divided into units of ten (an arban).** In battle, they would pretend to flee to make their enemy give chase. When the pursuing troops became disorganized the Mongols would turn on them, closing in to trap them.

**66** **The Battle of the Indus River was fought in 1221, in present-day Pakistan.** A Mongol army of 10,000 faced Muslim troops of 5,000 on the banks of the river. The Mongols inflicted heavy losses, and only a few Muslim soldiers crossed the river to safety.

◀ Mongol cavalrymen were expert archers. Some arrows they used made whistling noises and were used to send signals.

# Joan of Arc

**67** Born in France, Joan of Arc (1412–1431) lived at a time when large parts of France were controlled by the English. When Joan was about 12, she believed she had a vision in which the patron saints of France commanded her to dress as a man and lead the fight to rid France of the English.

▲ France, showing the area controlled by the English.

▼ Joan of Arc was easy to spot on the battlefield because she wore a suit of white armor.

**68** Joan lived during the Hundred Years' War. This was a series of wars between England and France that began in 1337. The wars were fought over English claims to be the rulers of France. Joan went to see France's *Dauphin* (crown prince), who was soon to become King Charles VII, and told him of her vision.

**69** Charles gave Joan permission to travel to the city of Orléans with a French army. The city was under siege from the English. The army arrived in April 1429. Joan was dressed as a knight, and carried a banner. Within a week, the English retreated. From then on, Joan was known as the "Maid of Orléans."

**70** For the next 12 months, Joan led the French in battles against the English. She won back territory for France. In May 1430, Joan was captured by the Duke of Burgundy (a French nobleman on the side of the English). She became a prisoner-of-war, and was eventually sold to the English.

▶ Saint Joan of Arc is one of the most popular saints of the Roman Catholic Church.

**71** The English put Joan on trial. She was tried as a witch and a heretic (a person who goes against the teachings of the Christian church), found guilty, and sentenced to death. In May 1431, Joan was burnt at the stake in the French city of Rouen. She was declared innocent 25 years after her death, and in 1920 the Pope made her a saint.

# Moctezuma

**72** **The Aztecs lived in the present-day country of Mexico.** They were fierce warriors who defeated rival tribes to become the strongest group in the region. The last Aztec emperor was called Moctezuma II (*c.*1480–1520). He became leader of the Aztecs in 1502. He was a powerful and ruthless leader who was feared and admired by his people.

▲ Moctezuma was regarded as a god by the Aztec people.

**73** **The Aztecs were a warlike people.** Every able-bodied man was expected to fight in Moctezuma's army. They were taught to use weapons as children, and at 15 they were old enough to go to war. It was considered an honor to fight for the emperor. Warriors who did well were rewarded with gifts of land and slaves.

**74** The fiercest Aztec fighters were the Eagle and Jaguar warriors. Eagle warriors wore suits made from feathers and Jaguar warriors dressed in ocelot skins. They were full-time soldiers, while the bulk of the army were part-time soldiers who returned to regular jobs after the fighting was over.

▶ A warrior's most important job was to capture prisoners for sacrifice. The more prisoners he took, the more important he became.

**75** Fighters fought with slings, bows and spears launched from spear-throwers. The most dangerous Aztec weapon was the war-club, the edges of which were covered with blades of razor-sharp obsidian (a glass-like stone made inside volcanoes). It could slice an enemy's head off in one blow.

▼ The Aztecs outnumbered the Spaniards, but the Spaniards had better weapons.

**76** In 1519, an army of Spaniards landed in Mexico in search of gold. When the news reached Moctezuma, he thought they were gods and sent them gifts, and when they first arrived in the Aztec capital he treated them as guests. He soon realized his mistake. Fighting between the Aztecs and the Spaniards began in May 1520. Moctezuma was killed, and the Aztec city was looted and destroyed.

Key

① Eagle warrior in a suit of feathers

② Fur and feather shield

③ Wooden club with shards of obsidian

④ Jaguar warrior

⑤ Spear tipped with obsidian

# Babur

**77** The founder of the Mughal Empire in northern India is known as Babur (1483–1531). His real name was Zahir ud-Din Muhammad, but as he rose to power he was given the nickname Babur, meaning "tiger." He was a powerful Muslim leader.

▲ The Battle of Khanwa (1527) gave Babur control of northern India.

◄ The extent of the Mughal empire in India.

**80** In the Battle of Panipat, Babur's warriors used gunpowder weapons called arquebuses. They were an early type of bullet-firing gun, and were the most up-to-date weapons of the time. The traditional weapons of Mughal warriors were a sword with a curved blade (*talwar*) and a mace. They wore chainmail armor and carried a small round shield (*dahl*).

**78** In 1504, Babur and a group of Muslim fighters captured Kabul, in Afghanistan. He established a small kingdom there, and began making raids into northern India. In 1525, he was asked to attack Ibrahim Lodi, the sultan (ruler) of Delhi, so Babur mounted a full-scale invasion of northern India.

▼►Weapons of Babur's Mughal warriors.

Mace

**79** Babur and Lodi's armies met at Panipat, India, in 1526. Babur had 25,000 troops, Lodi had 40,000. Lodi struck first, but failed to break through Babur's line of 700 carts tied together. After defeating Lodi's army, Babur marched to Delhi, which became the capital of the Mughal empire.

Knife

**81** **The largest part of Babur's army was the cavalry.** He could muster tens of thousands of horsemen, who served as archers, and were his elite troops. His foot soldiers were peasants who were forced to fight. Mughal armies also made use of war elephants, which acted as firing platforms for archers and spear-throwers. Because of their height, elephants were also used as command and observation posts.

**INVESTIGATE**

As well as being a warrior leader, Babur was also a poet, and his interest in nature led him to create magnificent gardens. Use books and the Internet to see if you can find out anything else about the founder of the Mughal Empire.

▶ War elephants were used by Mughal and other armies in India. Some elephants wore armor.

# Napoleon Bonaparte

**82** French general Napoleon Bonaparte (1769–1821) trained as a soldier from the age of ten. At 27 he was in charge of the French army in Italy. For a short time, he ruled a large part of Europe, creating the largest empire in Europe since the time of the Romans.

◀ Napoleon Bonaparte was a military genius, and one of the world's great generals.

**83** Napoleon fought by new rules. He marched his army at night, attacked in the rain and on Sundays, and ordered his troops to attack the enemy at their weakest point. He was young, ambitious and ruthless. In 1799 he overthrew the government of France, and became the country's new leader. In 1804 he organized his own coronation and became Emperor Napoleon.

▶ The Battle of Austerlitz. After his victory, Napoleon said to his troops: "Soldiers! I am pleased with you!"

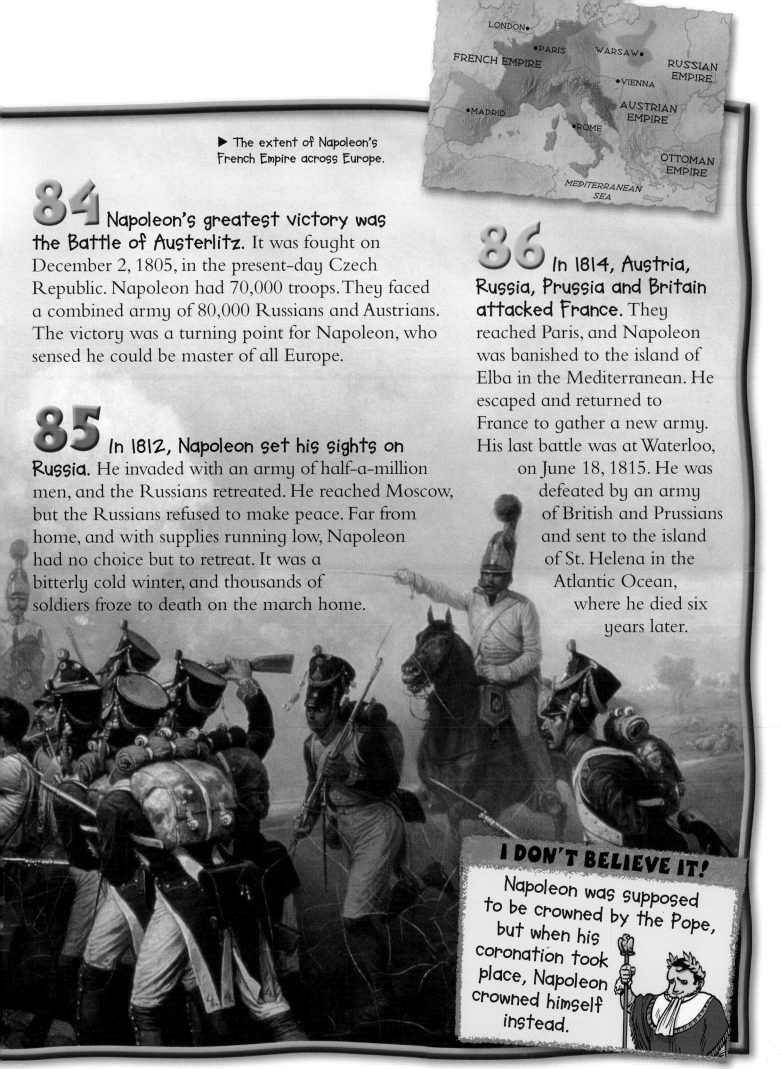

▶ The extent of Napoleon's French Empire across Europe.

LONDON
PARIS
FRENCH EMPIRE
WARSAW
RUSSIAN EMPIRE
VIENNA
MADRID
AUSTRIAN EMPIRE
ROME
OTTOMAN EMPIRE
MEDITERRANEAN SEA

**84** **Napoleon's greatest victory was the Battle of Austerlitz.** It was fought on December 2, 1805, in the present-day Czech Republic. Napoleon had 70,000 troops. They faced a combined army of 80,000 Russians and Austrians. The victory was a turning point for Napoleon, who sensed he could be master of all Europe.

**85** **In 1812, Napoleon set his sights on Russia.** He invaded with an army of half-a-million men, and the Russians retreated. He reached Moscow, but the Russians refused to make peace. Far from home, and with supplies running low, Napoleon had no choice but to retreat. It was a bitterly cold winter, and thousands of soldiers froze to death on the march home.

**86** **In 1814, Austria, Russia, Prussia and Britain attacked France.** They reached Paris, and Napoleon was banished to the island of Elba in the Mediterranean. He escaped and returned to France to gather a new army. His last battle was at Waterloo, on June 18, 1815. He was defeated by an army of British and Prussians and sent to the island of St. Helena in the Atlantic Ocean, where he died six years later.

**I DON'T BELIEVE IT!**

Napoleon was supposed to be crowned by the Pope, but when his coronation took place, Napoleon crowned himself instead.

# Shaka

**87** The first great chief of the Zulu nation in southern Africa was a warrior chieftain called Shaka (c. 1788–1828). He organized the army into regiments and gave his soldiers better weapons. Shaka made the Zulu nation the strongest in southern Africa.

**88** Before Shaka, the Zulu people were relatively peaceful. Battles were often wars of words. Shaka changed all this, bringing in stabbing spears and training his warriors to destroy their enemies. He organized campaigns against neighboring peoples, whom the Zulu either killed or forced to surrender.

**89** Zulu boys practiced fighting with sticks. At 18 they joined a regiment (*iButho*). Zulu warriors would sometimes fight duels with each other, swinging *iWisa* (clubs). It was seen as a way of making them tougher. In battle, they also used stabbing spears (*iklwa*), and throwing spears (*assegais*), and protected themselves with shields of cowhide.

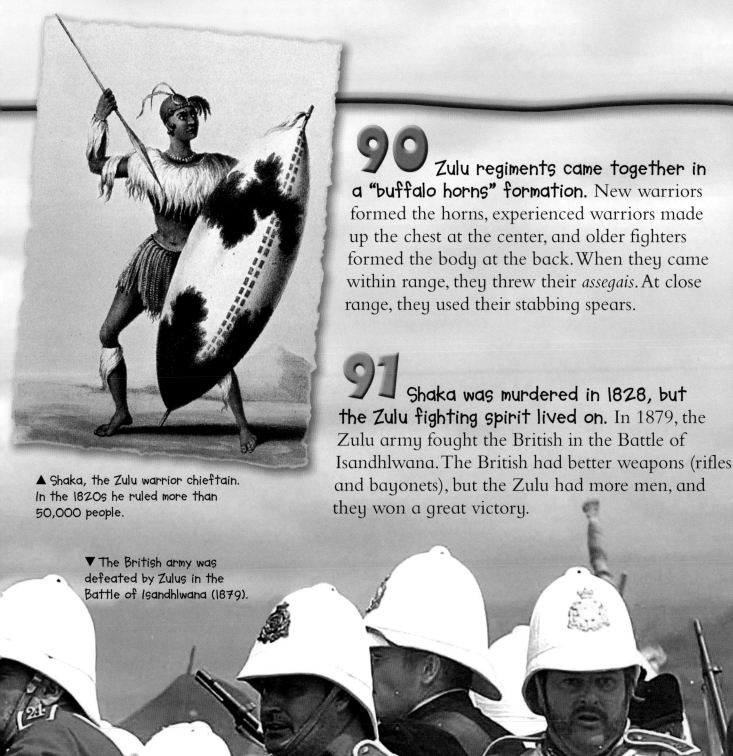

**90** Zulu regiments came together in a "buffalo horns" formation. New warriors formed the horns, experienced warriors made up the chest at the center, and older fighters formed the body at the back. When they came within range, they threw their *assegais*. At close range, they used their stabbing spears.

▲ Shaka, the Zulu warrior chieftain. In the 1820s he ruled more than 50,000 people.

**91** Shaka was murdered in 1828, but the Zulu fighting spirit lived on. In 1879, the Zulu army fought the British in the Battle of Isandhlwana. The British had better weapons (rifles and bayonets), but the Zulu had more men, and they won a great victory.

▼ The British army was defeated by Zulus in the Battle of Isandhlwana (1879).

QUIZ

1. What did Zulu boys practice fighting with?
2. What were Zulu clubs called?
3. What was the Zulu battle formation called?

Answers:
1. Sticks 2. iWisa 3. Buffalo horns

# Crazy Horse

**92** Crazy Horse (c. 1840–1877) was a Native American warrior chief. He belonged to the Oglala Sioux people and was involved in a struggle with the U.S. Army and white settlers. Crazy Horse wanted to stop them taking the Sioux land, and this led to a series of battles. He said he was "hostile to the white man" and that the Sioux wanted "peace and to be left alone."

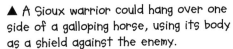

▲ A Sioux warrior could hang over one side of a galloping horse, using its body as a shield against the enemy.

◄ Crazy Horse was one of the greatest of all Native American war leaders.

**93** The traditional weapons of Sioux warriors were bows, lances and knives. When they came into contact with white settlers, they began trading for rifles and pistols. However, weapons were not their most prized possessions—horses were. The Sioux used horses for hunting and for war. Their horses were small and fast, and the Sioux were expert riders.

## QUIZ

1. Which native American tribe did Crazy Horse belong to?
2. What was a Sioux warrior's most prized possession?
3. In what year was the Battle of Little Big Horn?

Answers:
1. The Sioux
2. His horse 3. 1876

**95** From 1874, white settlers began moving into the Black Hills region of South Dakota, looking for gold. This was the ancestral homeland of the Sioux. The U.S. government ordered the Sioux to leave the area, but many refused to go. Crazy Horse called for Sioux warriors to fight, and they were joined by allies from the Cheyenne and Arapaho nations.

**94** As land was lost to white settlers, the Sioux began to act. Warbands of warriors began to make hit-and-run raids against U.S. Army outposts and isolated settlements. Stagecoaches and wagon trains carrying supplies were ambushed, and telegraph wires were cut. The U.S. Army found these tactics very difficult to fight. It was as if the Sioux were an invisible enemy.

▼ The Battle of the Little Bighorn is also known as Custer's Last Stand.

**96** The U.S. Army was sent to clear the area of Native Americans. Crazy Horse and other leaders brought more than 1,000 warriors together to resist them. On June 25 and 26, 1876, the Battle of the Little Bighorn was fought near the Little Bighorn River, Montana. A force of 700 soldiers of the U.S. Seventh Cavalry, led by General George Custer, was wiped out. Custer and a group of his men fought to the last on a small hill.

**97** Aragorn is a warrior in The Lord of the Rings trilogy of books, written by J.R.R. Tolkien. He first appeared in 1954, in *The Fellowship of the Ring* and is the leader of a group of heroes tasked with destroying a ring of great power. During their quest, he has to fight evil creatures such as orcs, goblins and the dreaded Nazgûl.

▼ Aragorn, as seen in the film version of the third book in the trilogy, *The Return of the King* (New Line Cinema, 2003).

**98** Link is a fantasy warrior from the Legend of Zelda video games. He was created by Shigeru Miyamoto, and was "born" in 1986. Link is portrayed as a brave warrior, who uses a magical sword, a boomerang, bombs and a bow.

▼ In the film *Star Wars Episode IV—A New Hope* (LucasFilm 1977) Jedi Master Obi-Wan Kenobi (left) and Darth Vader use their lightsabers in a duel.

**99** **The Jedi are warrior knights from the Star Wars films.** Their role is to keep peace in the universe, by using the forces of good to defeat evil. They fight with lightsabers—energy swords of colored light. The Jedi are organized into ranks. The most junior is a Jedi Youngling, and the most senior is a Jedi Grand Master.

**100** **Wolverine is a superhero ok character.** He first appeared in 1974. His skeleton is reinforced with adamantium—a super-strong metal that also forms his long claws, which can slice through metal and stone. He is a skilled fighter and his body heals itself with incredible speed.

▲ Wolverine is one of a group of heroes called the "X-men" who use their super physical and mental powers to fight evil and protect ordinary people.

# Index

Entries in **bold** refer to main subject entries. Entries in *italics* refer to illustrations.